ANCIENT EGYPT

THE HISTORY
DETECTIVE
INVESTIGATES

Rachel Minay

WAYLAND

First published in 2014 by Wayland

Copyright © Wayland 2014

Wayland
338 Euston Road
London NW1 3BH

Wayland Australia
Level 17/207 Kent Street
Sydney, NSW 2000

The History Detective Investigates series:

Produced for Wayland by
White-Thomson Publishing Ltd
www.wtpub.co.uk
+44 (0)843 208 7460

Editor: Rachel Minay
Designer: Ian Winton
Cover design concept: Lisa Peacock
Consultant: Philip Parker
Proofreader: Lucy Ross

A catalogue record for this title is available from the British Library.

ISBN: 978-0-7502-8179-9
eBook ISBN: 978-0-7502-8562-9

Dewey Number: 932-dc23

Printed in Malaysia

10 9 8 7 6 5 4 3 2 1

Wayland is a division of Hachette Children's Books, an Hachette UK company

Picture Acknowledgments: Stefan Chabluk: 4t; **Shutterstock:** cover t (Dan Breckwoldt), 4b (S-F), 6 (Asta Plechaviciute), 8t (Matej Kastelic), 8b (Vladimir Wrangel), 11b (mountainpix), 14t (airphoto.gr), 14b (Marcin Sylwia Ciesielski), 16 (MAEADV), 17t (meunierd), 18t (Nestor Noci), 18b (Jose Ignacio Soto), 22 (Dan Breckwoldt), 23t (Pius Lee), 25b (nagib), 26t (Kamira), 27 (mountainpix), 28 (meunierd); **Topfoto:** 11t (AAAC); **Werner Forman Archive:** cover b (Egyptian Museum, Cairo. Location: 44), 7t, 9 (Egyptian Museum, Cairo. Location: 44), 10 (Dr E. Strouhal. Location: 101), 12 (Hermitage Museum, St Petersburg. Location: 45), 13t (British Museum, London. Location: 36), 19 (The Louvre, Paris. Location: 51), 20t (Egyptian Museum, Cairo. Location: 44); **Wikimedia:** 1 (Marie-Lan Nguyen), 3 (Janmad), 5 (Marcus Cyron), 7b (Carole Raddato), 13b, 15t (Janmad), 15b (Hans Hillewaert), 17b (Gerbil), 20b (Walters Art Museum), 21t, 21b, 23b (en:User:Chipdawes), 24, 25t (Σταύρος), 26b (Sotheby's New York, 05 Mai 2011, lot 65), 29t, 29b (José-Manuel Benito).

Above: This mask was to cover the face of an ancient Egyptian **mummy**.

Previous page: This rich piece of jewellery, called a pectoral, is made from gold, glass and turquoise, a semi-precious stone.

Cover (top): The pyramids at Giza.

Cover (bottom): Detail from Tutankhamun's throne.

CONTENTS

Words in **bold** can be found in the glossary on page 30.

The history detective Sherlock Bones will help you to find clues and collect evidence about ancient Egypt. Wherever you see one of Sherlock's paw-prints, you will find a mystery to solve. The answers are on page 31.

WHO WERE THE ANCIENT EGYPTIANS?

Egypt lies in the north of Africa, between the Mediterranean and Red Seas. Most of the country is hot, dry desert, but it is also home to the Nile, the longest river on earth. About 6,000 years ago, an amazing ancient civilization started to grow on the banks of the River Nile.

Farmers first settled on the banks of the Nile around 5000 BCE. In early times, Egypt was split into two kingdoms called Upper Egypt and Lower Egypt. Then, in 3100 BCE, the king of Upper Egypt, probably called Narmer, conquered Lower Egypt and ruled one united kingdom with a capital city at Memphis.

Historians divide ancient Egyptian history into different periods. The greatest achievements of the Egyptians date from three main periods: the Old Kingdom (about 2686-2181 BCE), the Middle Kingdom (about 2055-1650 BCE) and the New Kingdom (about 1550-1069 BCE). The pyramids (see pages 22-23) date from the Old Kingdom. During the Middle Kingdom, the capital city moved from Memphis to Thebes. The famous **pharaohs** Tutankhamun and Ramesses II lived during the New Kingdom. These periods of time are further divided up into **dynasties**, or families of pharaohs.

MEDITERRANEAN SEA
ROSETTA
ALEXANDRIA
AVARIS
GIZA
SAQQARA
MEMPHIS
LOWER EGYPT
AMARNA
DENDERA
THEBES
(LUXOR AND KARNAK)
UPPER EGYPT
ASWAN
RED SEA
LOWER NUBIA
ABU SIMBEL
NILE RIVER

The main sites in ancient Egypt were all built on the banks of the Nile.

The ancient Egyptians were incredible architects and builders. The Great Pyramid at Giza was one of the seven wonders of the ancient world and is the only one of the seven still standing.

We know a lot about the ancient Egyptians because of what they left behind. Pyramids and temples were built from stone because they were intended to last forever. The Egyptians believed in an afterlife so they filled tombs with objects they thought would be needed after death. These buildings and objects, together with paintings and **hieroglyphs**, tell us about the daily lives and beliefs of the people.

The Egyptians nearly always painted people with their heads and legs in profile, but with their shoulders and chest (and the eye you can see) as if from the front. Beautiful tomb paintings like this tell us about ancient Egyptian life.

This painting shows a man called Nebamun hunting birds in the marshes with his wife and daughter. What other animals can you spot?

Perhaps most amazingly of all, the Egyptians **preserved** themselves through mummification (see pages 20-21). Sculptures and paintings show us striking images of ancient Egyptians and their mummies bring us face to face with the people themselves.

DETECTIVE WORK

Explore the famous sites of ancient Egypt and then test yourself with a quiz at: www.childrensuniversity. manchester.ac.uk/ interactives/history/egypt/ egyptianmap/

WHY WAS THE RIVER NILE IMPORTANT?

The River Nile was vital to the development and growth of ancient Egypt. Its waters made farming, travel and trade possible. Nearly all Egyptian cities were built on its banks.

Once a year, between the middle of June and October, the Nile burst its banks and flooded. This spread a thick, black mud called silt over the land either side of the river, making it **fertile**. The Egyptians **irrigated** the land by building canals from the river to bring water to different parts of the farmers' fields. Because the black soil left by the flooding brought food and wealth to Egypt, black was a lucky colour for the Egyptians and represented 'life'. In contrast, red – the colour of the dry, lifeless desert that covered the rest of the country – represented 'death'.

This photo shows the Nile near Aswan. Plants can grow in the fertile valley, but not in the nearby desert dunes.

DETECTIVE WORK

Find out more facts about the River Nile at: http://resources.woodlands-junior.kent.sch.uk/homework/egypt/nile.htm

The ancient Greek historian Herodotus called Egypt the 'gift of the river'. This is how he described the annual flood:

'When the Nile comes over the land… the rest of Egypt becomes a sea and the cities alone rise above water.'

The farmer's year was based around this annual flood. In autumn, once the flood had passed, farmers ploughed the ground and sowed their crops. These included barley and wheat, which were made into bread, beer and cakes, as well as grapes, melons, beans and other vegetables. Between March and May, the crops were harvested. During the flood, farmers couldn't work their land, although they might have to work on the building of pyramids or temples for the pharaoh.

Grapes grew well on the banks of the Nile. In this painting, Egyptians are harvesting grapes, trampling them to get the juice out and storing the wine they have made.

There were not many roads in ancient Egypt – the Nile was the main route for travelling and for transporting goods. People had simple boats, made from **papyrus** reeds, for fishing. They used wooden boats for trade and to carry the vast quantities of stone needed for the pharaoh's building projects.

The Nile made life in Egypt possible, but the people who lived on its banks had to be careful it didn't bring death, too! Hippos and crocodiles were a dangerous part of river life but were also worshipped – the goddess of pregnancy and childbirth, Tawaret, had the body of a hippopotamus and the tail of a crocodile.

🐾 **The painting shows the winemaking process, but in the wrong order. Which part of the picture shows which part of the process?**

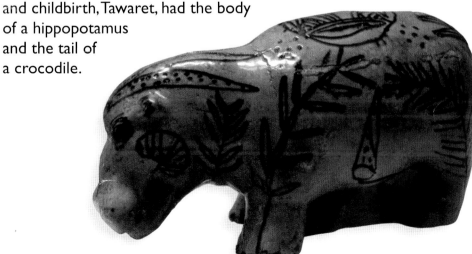

This figure of a hippopotamus, decorated with water plants as if it is in the river, dates from about 1650-1550 BCE.

WHO WERE THE PHARAOHS?

The pharaoh was the king of Egypt. The word 'pharaoh' meant 'great house' and originally described the king's palace. But 'great house' is also a good way to explain how the ancient Egyptians saw the pharaoh, because they thought the spirit of the gods lived in the king's human form. Pharaohs were seen as gods themselves and they were very powerful.

These statues of Hatshepsut at her tomb show her dressed as Osiris, god of the underworld, who was usually depicted as a mummified man.

Although the vast majority of pharaohs were men, there were a few women who ruled ancient Egypt. Hatshepsut was the stepmother of the baby Pharaoh Thutmose III but ruled herself from 1473 to 1458 BCE. To strengthen her position, she encouraged the idea that she was the daughter of the god Amun and ruled as a 'male' pharaoh. For example, she was written about as 'he' and shown in pictures dressed as a man with a false beard!

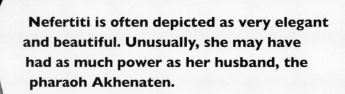

Another powerful female figure was Nefertiti, queen of Akhenaten, who ruled from 1352 to 1336 BCE. The Egyptians had always believed in many gods, but Akhenaten decided that one should be worshipped above all others (see page 17). The art from this period is also strikingly different. People were depicted with long, thin features rather than the strong, solid ones seen on the statues of previous pharaohs.

Nefertiti is often depicted as very elegant and beautiful. Unusually, she may have had as much power as her husband, the pharaoh Akhenaten.

The pharaoh who followed Akhenaten (and now known to be his son) was Tutankhamun. He became king at the age of eight or nine and only ruled until his death at the age of about eighteen, but he is the most well known of all Egyptian pharaohs because his tomb lay undiscovered until 1922. When it was unearthed by the **archaeologist** Howard Carter, it caused a sensation because it was almost **intact** and filled with thousands of treasures. Amazingly – and probably because it was very small for a pharaoh's tomb and well hidden – it had not been emptied by robbers like many other Egyptian tombs.

🐾 **Why was the discovery of Tutankhamun's tomb so unusual?**

The mask of Tutankhamun's mummy is made from gold, glass and semi-precious stones.

Howard Carter spent five years looking for Tutankhamun's tomb and a further eight years to clear it. This is how he described the moment he broke through into the burial chamber:

'I inserted an electric torch. An astonishing sight its light revealed, for there, within a yard of the doorway, stretching as far as one could see and blocking the entrance to the chamber, stood what to all appearances was a solid wall of gold.'

A pharaoh usually had one main wife, the queen, and other wives. Ramesses II was a long-lived pharaoh who ruled from 1279 to 1213 BCE and died at the age of ninety-six. He is thought to have had many wives and around 100 children! Known as 'Ramesses the Great', he was a military leader who also built some extraordinary buildings, such as the temples at Abu Simbel (see page 18).

DETECTIVE WORK

How did Carter find the tomb of Tutankhamun and what is the 'Mummy's Curse'? Find out at: http://resources.woodlands-junior.kent.sch.uk/homework/tut.html

WHAT WAS DAILY LIFE LIKE?

Although the pharaoh and the noble families of ancient Egypt enjoyed great wealth and power, most people were peasants. Family life was very important to all Egyptians, and animals also played a large part in daily life.

Egyptian families were often very large, with many children and several generations living in the same house. Children were considered to be adults from the age of twelve and girls often married in their early teens. The Egyptians tended to have fun at home, rather than going to large public entertainments like the ancient Greeks and Romans. They liked playing board games, as well as games we still know today such as leap frog and tug-of-war.

DETECTIVE WORK

Compare and contrast the daily life of a nobleman with that of a farmer in ancient Egypt at: http://www.ancientegypt.co.uk/life/story/main.html

It was important to keep cool in the hot Egyptian climate. Houses were made from mud bricks and had small windows. The very poor lived in huts built from reeds. Clothes were made of linen, a fabric woven from a plant called flax. Women usually wore a long, loose dress, while men wore a shorter kilt or **loincloth**. Rich people had their clothes pressed into pleats. Children usually wore nothing.

This tomb painting shows a family group. Children usually had partly shaved heads with a curl of hair, called 'the side-lock of youth', hanging down.

🐾 **Egypt is a very hot country. What would have helped to keep this garden cool and shady?**

Wealthy people had larger homes with gardens designed around a pool.

Both women and men cared about their appearance. They bathed regularly and wore makeup and perfume. The distinctive eye makeup we see on so many pictures of the ancient Egyptians was made from **minerals**. It could be black or green and was probably worn as protection against disease or the sun. The heat meant that people wore their hair short but wigs were common for special occasions. All Egyptians loved wearing jewellery: the rich wore gold and precious stones; the poor wore beads and cheaper metals such as copper.

This delicate carving shows two Egyptians wearing wigs, necklaces and eye makeup.

The ancient Egyptians had a close relationship with animals. They raised livestock and hunted animals for food, but they also kept many animals as pets, including cats, dogs and monkeys. Egyptian gods and goddesses (see pages 16-17) often took a partly animal form.

The ancient Greek historian Herodotus was surprised that when there was a fire, the Egyptians were more worried about their cats than putting out the fire! He said:

'... *the Egyptians stand at intervals and look after the cats, not taking any care to extinguish the fire, the cats slipping through or leaping over the men, jump into the fire; and when this happens, great* **mourning** *comes upon the Egyptians.*'

HoW DID THE ANCIENT EGYPTIANS MAKE A LIVING?

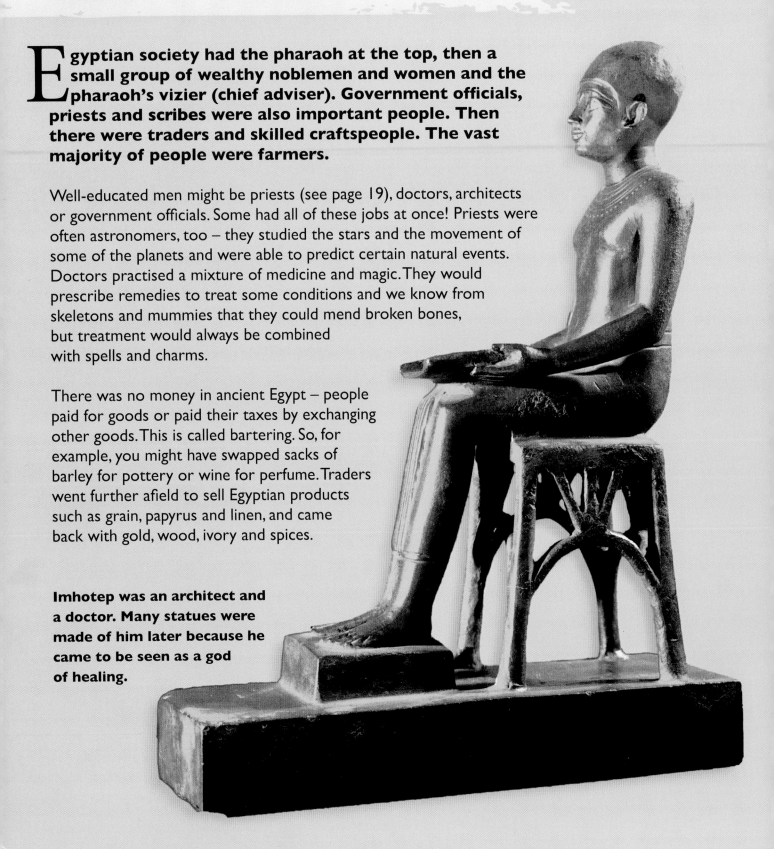

Egyptian society had the pharaoh at the top, then a small group of wealthy noblemen and women and the pharaoh's vizier (chief adviser). Government officials, priests and scribes were also important people. Then there were traders and skilled craftspeople. The vast majority of people were farmers.

Well-educated men might be priests (see page 19), doctors, architects or government officials. Some had all of these jobs at once! Priests were often astronomers, too – they studied the stars and the movement of some of the planets and were able to predict certain natural events. Doctors practised a mixture of medicine and magic. They would prescribe remedies to treat some conditions and we know from skeletons and mummies that they could mend broken bones, but treatment would always be combined with spells and charms.

There was no money in ancient Egypt – people paid for goods or paid their taxes by exchanging other goods. This is called bartering. So, for example, you might have swapped sacks of barley for pottery or wine for perfume. Traders went further afield to sell Egyptian products such as grain, papyrus and linen, and came back with gold, wood, ivory and spices.

Imhotep was an architect and a doctor. Many statues were made of him later because he came to be seen as a god of healing.

The number of beautiful objects archaeologists have found in Egyptian tombs tells us there were many skilled craftspeople in ancient times. The vast and lifelike images of pharaohs and the fantastic paintings found in tombs and temples were created by talented sculptors and artists. Crafts included fine metalwork, pottery and carpentry.

Most Egyptian women worked in the home and brought up children. A few were priestesses or worked as musicians or dancers. Women from poor families might work as weavers or servants.

The musicians in this painting are wearing cones on the top of their heads that are often shown in Egyptian paintings. They are thought to be cones of wax that would slowly melt to keep the wearer cool and perfumed.

This beautifully decorated glass fish dates from 1352-1336 BCE. It was probably used to hold cosmetics or special oil.

DETECTIVE WORK

Discover more about the craftspeople of ancient Egypt and explore two workshops at: http://www.ancientegypt.co.uk/trade/home.html

What is unusual about the way the two musicians on the right have been painted?

WHAT ARE HIEROGLYPHS?

The ancient Egyptians did not write in words using an alphabet like ours. Instead, they wrote in hieroglyphs – a form of picture writing. Hieroglyphs are like a secret code to the lives of these ancient people.

Hieroglyphs did not have to be read left to right like our writing. They could also go top to bottom or right to left! This made it easier for the ancient Egyptians to fit writing around their artwork.

Some hieroglyphs stood for letters or sounds; others stood for whole words or ideas. For example, the **ankh** was an important symbol that meant 'life'. The direction the animals or people faced told the reader which way to read the writing. If they faced left, then you read from left to right; if they faced right, then you read from right to left.

▼ The name of a king or queen was often put into a special shape called a **cartouche**.

Cartouche of Ramesses III

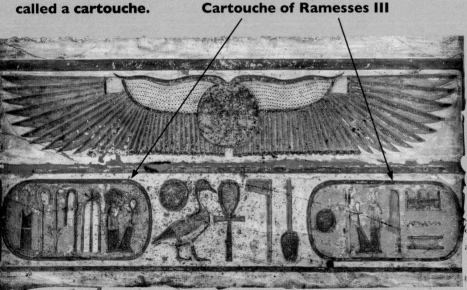

🐾 The ankh hieroglyph looks a bit like a cross with a loop at the top. Can you find it on the picture?

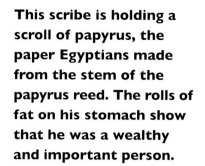

Most people in ancient Egypt could not read or write. Children did not usually go to school because they were helping their families instead and because it was not free to go to school. Boys from noble families might go to a temple school from the age of about five. They would learn to read and write hieroglyphs and often grew up to work as scribes.

Scribes were people whose job it was to write things down. It took a long time to become a scribe because there were more than 700 hieroglyphs to learn. Scribes kept important records for the government and also wrote down stories about the pharaohs.

Many examples of ancient Egyptian hieroglyphs have survived, but for hundreds of years historians were unable to **decipher** them. Then, in 1799, a stone slab was found near Rosetta, a city near to the Mediterranean coast. It showed an official order from the king written in three different ways, including Egyptian hieroglyphs and ancient Greek. People already understood the ancient Greek, so they could now understand the hieroglyphs – which said the same thing – for the first time.

This scribe is holding a scroll of papyrus, the paper Egyptians made from the stem of the papyrus reed. The rolls of fat on his stomach show that he was a wealthy and important person.

DETECTIVE WORK

Learn more about hieroglyphs and how to write in them at: http://www.childrensuniversity.manchester.ac.uk/interactives/history/egypt/hieroglyphs/

The Rosetta Stone helped to unlock the secrets of Egyptian hieroglyphs. It took a long time, though – more than twenty years.

WHO WERE THE EGYPTIAN GODS AND GODDESSES?

The ancient Egyptians worshipped hundreds of gods and goddesses. Most took a half-animal, half-human form. Pharaohs were seen as providing a link to the gods and were also considered to be gods themselves.

This table shows some of the many Egyptian gods and goddesses.

DETECTIVE WORK

Discover more about Egyptian gods at the British Museum site and play the 'Challenge' to speak to statues of the gods and help someone escape from the museum! http://www.ancientegypt. co.uk/gods/home.html

Name	Role	Animal form
Amun	king of the gods, sometimes combined with the sun god to be Amun-Ra	ram; also shown as a man wearing a tall hat made from ostrich feathers
Ra (or Re)	sun god	falcon wearing a headdress with the sun's disk
Thoth	moon god of writing and wisdom	ibis (a bird) or baboon
Horus	sky god and protector of the pharaoh	falcon
Anubis	god of death and mummification	jackal
Isis	mother goddess who had magical powers	
Osiris	god of the underworld	
Hathor	protective goddess and goddess of music, love and happiness	cow
Bastet	protective goddess	cat
Tawaret	goddess of pregnancy and childbirth	hippo with the tail of a crocodile

Which Egyptian goddess do you think this statue represents?

The ancient Egyptians believed that the gods controlled all of nature, as well as people. They also used the gods and goddesses to explain the mysteries of the natural world. For example, they thought that the sun god, Ra, sailed his boat across the sky in the day and travelled through the underworld at night. They believed a star-covered goddess called Nut protected the sky.

Only during the reign of Akhenaten and Nefertiti did this worship of many gods change. Akhenaten's radical belief in worshipping a single god – the Aten or sun-disk – must have seemed shocking to the people of Egypt. After his death, they gradually returned to their old beliefs.

This is an image of Thoth, the god of writing and the moon. Some people think that the curved beak of the ibis looks similar to a crescent moon.

This limestone carving shows Akhenaten, Nefertiti and their children, with the rays of the Aten shining down on them. The natural style of this family portrait was unusual during other periods of Egyptian art.

These lines are from a longer poem called *The Great Hymn to the Aten*, thought to have been written by Akhenaten himself:

'You rise beautiful from the
horizon on heaven,
living disk, origin of life.
You are arisen from the
horizon,
you have filled every land
with your beauty.'

WHAT WERE THE SECRETS OF THE TEMPLE?

The Egyptians built vast stone temples to their gods and goddesses. Many have survived so we know a lot about them. However, in ancient times, very few people saw inside these secret buildings.

The ancient Egyptians believed temples were homes for their gods to live in on earth. At the entrance was a massive gate called a **pylon**, often decorated with pictures of the gods or of the pharaoh fighting battles. Tall pillars called **obelisks** and impressive statues of the pharaoh stood in front of the pylon. At certain times, such as festivals, ordinary people were allowed through the gateway into the temple courtyard – but no further. So what lay beyond?

Ramesses II built more temples than any other pharaoh, including the magnificent ones at Abu Simbel. The four colossal statues are of Ramesses himself.

▼ Over time, people who love Egyptian art have taken pieces away – even huge obelisks! The missing obelisk from Luxor Temple is now in the centre of Paris.

Obelisk

Statue of the pharaoh

Pylon

The **hypostyle hall** was a large room filled with masses of columns. These were necessary to hold up the heavy stone roof, but were probably also **symbolic** of plants that existed when the world was created. Beyond the hall there were further rooms that led to the darkest and most secret part of the temple, the **sanctuary**. This is where the statue of the temple god was kept and only the pharaoh and high priests were allowed in.

Priests were very important people. They had to carry out temple **rituals**, such as bringing offerings of food to the god's statue, at certain times of the day. If ordinary people wished to ask the god a question about something, the priests would answer on their behalf. You can imagine that this gave them a lot of power and at some points in Egyptian history, high priests wanted – and may have had – as much power as the pharaoh.

DETECTIVE WORK

Ordinary people couldn't go into the secret heart of the temple – but you can! Discover the secrets for yourself at: http://www.ancientegypt.co.uk/temples/story/main.html

🐾 **Most ancient Egyptian paintings show people dressed in white linen clothes, but the priestess' dress looks different. What do you think it might be made from?**

Most priests were men but noblewomen could become priestesses. This shows a princess called Nefertiabet dressed as a priestess.

WHAT IS MUMMIFICATION?

The ancient Egyptians believed that a person needed their body after death. Therefore they thought it was important to preserve the body through mummification.

Making a mummy was the job of an **embalmer** and it was a complicated process that took about seventy days. First the body was washed. Then the lungs, stomach, intestines and liver were removed, dried and placed into one of four special containers called **Canopic jars**. The heart was left in the body because the Egyptians believed it would be weighed in the afterlife.

The brain was pulled out by putting a hook up the person's nose. A salt-like substance called natron was used to dry out the body, which was then left for about forty days. It was then washed, oiled and stuffed with linen and sawdust. Finally, the mummy was wrapped in up to twenty layers of linen and put in a coffin. Small pieces of jewellery called amulets were often slipped into the layers in the hope of keeping evil away.

This Canopic chest and jars were found in Tutankhamun's tomb.

DETECTIVE WORK

Learn more about embalming by playing the mummy maker game at: http://www.bbc.co.uk/history/ancient/egyptians/launch_gms_mummy_maker.shtml

The mummy's face would be covered by a painted mask. Together with the coffin, the mask was thought to help protect the dead person as they journeyed through the underworld.

SO W

Mummification was important because the Egyptians believed that the dead person's spirit would return to its body after travelling to the underworld. The person's heart would be 'weighed' by Anubis against the feather of Maat, the goddess of truth and justice. If their heart was too heavy, it would be eaten by Ammut, a creature that was part lion, part crocodile and part hippopotamus. The person would not go on to live in the afterlife.

To begin with, only pharaohs were mummified, but over time it became usual for any Egyptian who could afford it. But it wasn't only people who were preserved in this way. The Egyptians loved their pets so much that they were often prepared for the afterlife, too, and wild animals were mummified as gifts for the gods. By the end of the Egyptian period, making all kinds of animal mummies – from tiny beetles to giant crocodiles – was big business.

Once the mummy was ready, the 'opening of the mouth' ritual was performed. A priest touched the person's mouth so they would be able to speak, eat and drink in the afterlife.

▼ **This scene shows Anubis weighing the heart of Ani, a scribe. Ammut waits in case Ani fails the test.**

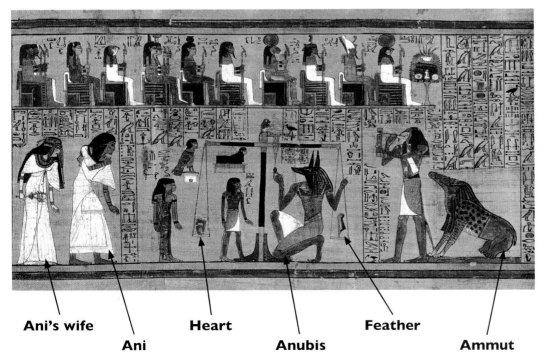

Ani's wife   Heart   Feather

    Ani   Anubis   Ammut

🐾 **Who is the god on the left of Ammut? (Clue: Look back at page 16.)**

WHY WERE THE PYRAMIDS BUILT?

The pyramids are some of the oldest and most amazing buildings in the world. There are many pyramids in Egypt but the biggest and most impressive are the group of three built at Giza, on the west bank of the Nile.

The pyramids at Giza were built as massive tombs for three pharaohs – Khufu, Khafre and Menkaure. The mummified body of each pharaoh was placed in the burial chamber, deep in the heart of the pyramid. This was to protect it from the hot sun and from grave robbers. The ancient Egyptians put many other things in too, such as food, furniture and pets, because they believed the dead person would need these in the afterlife.

Thousands of workers were needed to build Khufu's Great Pyramid. Between 5,000 and 20,000 worked on the building of the pyramid, most of them farmers who were called up to work during the flood season. It took about twenty years and 2.3 million blocks of stone to build it. Originally, the pyramids were covered in a smooth surface of white limestone, which would have been dazzlingly bright under the Egyptian sun.

DETECTIVE WORK

Build a pyramid at: http://www.bbc.co.uk/history/ancient/egyptians/launch_gms_pyramid_builder.shtml and explore a hidden tomb at: http://www.nms.ac.uk/education/games_and_fun/egyptian_tomb_adventure.aspx

Khufu's pyramid is the biggest but looks smaller because it is on lower ground. At 146 m (481 ft) high, it was the tallest building in the world for thousands of years – it is thought to have been beaten by Lincoln Cathedral in about 1300 CE.

Khafre

Menkaure

Khufu

Khafre was the son of Khufu. He is associated with the Great **Sphinx**, a vast statue that stands close to the three pyramids. The largest sculpture ever built by an ancient civilization, the Sphinx is 60 m (200 ft) long and 20 m (65 ft) high.

The head of the Great Sphinx may be a portrait of Pharaoh Khafre.

🐾 Most of the smooth limestone that once covered the pyramids has been taken away and used on other buildings. Some remains on Khafre's pyramid – can you see where it is?

The third pyramid at Giza was built by Menkaure, who was Khafre's son. This statue of him shows the typical representation of the ideal god-like pharaoh.

We don't fully understand why the pyramid shape was so important to the ancient Egyptians. It may have been that it helped the pharaoh travel 'up to the stars' and it may also have been to do with the worship of the sun – each pyramid lies almost exactly east-west.

Because pyramids contained many riches, they were often looted by robbers. Also, the huge amount of work that went into building a pyramid would have been very expensive. Eventually, the ancient Egyptians stopped building pyramids and instead built secret tombs for their dead.

'Man fears time, but time fears the pyramids.'

Arab proverb.

DID THE ANCIENT EGYPTIANS FIGHT WARS?

For many years in its history, Egypt was not a warlike nation and did not have an army. At other times, especially when it tried to expand its territory or had to protect itself from attack, it had a large and well-organized army.

Nubia was a country that lay to the south of Egypt and it had valuable **natural resources**, such as gold and semi-precious stones. Egypt traded with Nubia but, at various times in its history, it also attacked its neighbour for control of this wealth. During the Middle Kingdom period, the powerful pharaoh Senusret III waged war on Nubia at least four times and built river forts in the south.

At the end of the Middle Kingdom, the Egyptians went from being invaders to being invaded themselves, as the Hyksos took over much of Egypt and made their capital at Avaris. The Hyksos came from the Levant (modern-day Israel, Jordan, Lebanon and Syria). For 200 years, Egypt battled to throw the Hyksos out; this was finally achieved by Ahmose I in about 1550 BCE.

DETECTIVE WORK

Find out more about warfare in ancient Egypt at:
http://www.historyforkids.org/learn/egypt/war/

This carving is thought to show Narmer, the first king of all Egypt. He is in the traditional pose of a warlike pharaoh, striking or 'smiting' a prisoner. The men below are either fleeing for their lives or lying dead.

The army was often led into battles by the pharaoh. One of the most powerful military pharaohs was Ramesses II, or Ramesses the Great. Pictures often show him fighting against the Hittites (ancient Turks) at the Battle of Kadesh in 1274 BCE. Ramesses' son, Merenptah, also saw battle – this time against Libyans from the Western Desert and a group known as the Sea Peoples. Ramesses III, who reigned from 1184 to 1153 BCE, also fought and defeated the Libyans and the Sea Peoples, but he was to be the last of the strong pharaoh-gods that had dominated the country for so long. Victory in war would soon be a thing of the past – Egypt was beginning to crumble.

The life of a soldier in ancient Egypt was hard:

*'He carries his bread and his water on his shoulders like an ass's burden; his spine is dislocated. He drinks **brackish** water and sleeps with one eye open… When the time comes for him to return to Egypt he is like a worm-eaten piece of wood.'*

Egyptologist Pierre Montet, quoting from an ancient text.

◀ **The Egyptian army was made up of foot soldiers, like these, and chariots. Foot soldiers used weapons such as battle-axes and spears, but did not wear much armour and went barefoot.**

▶ **The ancient Egyptians often used war chariots in battle. Pictures tend to show pharaohs riding in chariots alone, but there would usually have been two people: one to drive and one to shoot arrows at the enemy.**

🐾 **Why do you think pictures showed the pharaoh in a chariot alone if there were usually two people in a chariot?**

YOUR PROJECT

You now know a lot about the history and achievements of the ancient Egyptians. Which aspect of Egyptian life would you like to research in depth for your project?

Perhaps you could draw up a timeline of the main events in ancient Egypt, from the first settlers along the Nile to the defeat by the Romans in 30 BCE. Alternatively, you could study one person in depth, such as Ramesses the Great, Akhenaten or Cleopatra. You could find out more about the archaeologist Howard Carter and his incredible discovery of Tutankhamun's tomb (do you think there's any truth in the story of the 'Mummy's Curse'?).

You could focus on any of the topics covered in this book, for example the different gods and goddesses, warfare or mummification. You could research one of the ancient sites, such as the pyramids at Giza or the Valley of the Kings, where many pharaohs were buried. Or perhaps you are more interested in the daily lives of ordinary Egyptians? You could find out more about what kinds of food people ate or what games they played.

For a creative task, you could look more closely at Egyptian art and create a piece in the same style, showing people partly in profile. What event or aspect of daily life will you show? Could you add any Egyptian hieroglyphs or design your own?

The 'Step Pyramid' at Saqqara is the earliest stone pyramid in Egypt. Imhotep (see page 12) is said to have been the architect.

You could write an imaginary diary for a farmer – perhaps one who has been called up to work on one of the pharaoh's building projects.

Project presentation

- Do plenty of research for your project. Use the Internet and your local or school library. If you live near London, you might be able to visit the British Museum, but if not you can visit the website: http://www.ancientegypt.co.uk

- If you are writing a biography of an ancient Egyptian, imagine what questions you would ask them and what they might answer.

- Collect as many pictures as you can to illustrate your project. Print off images from the Internet or draw items that you see in museums. Will your project need a map or timeline?

Ancient Egyptian sculpture, such as this portrait of Khafre, can be very powerful. Find examples in books or on the Internet.

GLOSSARY

ankh A symbol that looks like a cross with a loop at the top and meaning 'life' in ancient Egypt.

archaeologist Someone who studies the remains of past societies.

architect Someone who designs buildings.

BCE 'Before the Common Era'. Used to signify years before the believed birth of Jesus, around 2,000 years ago.

brackish Slightly salty.

Canopic jar A covered jar used to hold the organs of an embalmed body.

cartouche An oval or oblong shape containing hieroglyphs, usually the name of a pharaoh.

CE 'Common Era'. Used to signify years since the believed birth of Jesus.

decipher Decode or understand.

dune A mound of sand formed by the wind.

dynasty A line of rulers from the same family.

embalmer Someone who preserves a dead body to stop it rotting away.

fertile Able to produce a lot of plants or crops.

hieroglyph A picture that represents a word or sound in ancient Egyptian writing.

hypostyle hall A room where the roof is supported by pillars or columns.

intact Complete and undamaged.

irrigate Supply plants with water.

loincloth A piece of cloth wrapped around the hips.

mineral A solid substance that occurs naturally.

mourning Deep sadness when someone has died.

mummy A dead body that has been preserved and wrapped in bandages.

natural resources Useful materials that occur naturally, such as wood, coal or gold.

obelisk A stone pillar.

papyrus A material made from a water plant that was used for writing on and to make items such as boats.

pharaoh The person who ruled in ancient Egypt.

preserve Keep something as it is or treat it in a certain way to stop it from rotting or decaying.

profile An outline of something as seen from one side.

pylon In ancient Egypt, the gateway to a temple, made up of two towers.

ritual A ceremony, often a religious one.

sanctuary The holiest part of a temple.

scribe Someone whose job it is to write things down.

sphinx A stone figure with the body of a lion and the head of a person or animal.

symbolic Used to describe something that represents or stands for something else.

valley A low area of land between hills.

ANSWERS

Page 5:   Apart from many different kinds of birds, there are also butterflies in the air and fish in the water below him. Well done if you also managed to spot the ginger cat to the left of his leg – it is very well camouflaged!

Page 7:   Left – trampling the grapes; centre – storing the wine in jars; right – harvesting the grapes.

Page 9:   The discovery was unusual because the tomb was almost intact and full of priceless treasures.

Page 11:   The pool is surrounded by trees so the shade would have helped to keep the garden cool.

Page 13:   Their faces are shown from the front rather than in profile. This is very unusual in Egyptian art.

Page 14:   The ankh is right in the middle of the row of hieroglyphs.

Page 16:   Bastet, because she is represented as a cat.

Page 19:   The dress is made from animal skin (it is actually the skin of a black-spotted panther).

Page 21:   It is Thoth, because he has the head of an ibis and also he is writing something down.

Page 23:   The limestone can still be seen at the top of Khafre's pyramid.

Page 25:   It would make the pharaoh look like a strong leader and a hero in battle.

FURTHER INFORMATION

Books to read
Ancient Egypt (Navigators) by Miranda Smith (Kingfisher, 2010)
Everything Ancient Egypt by Crispin Boyer (National Geographic Kids, 2012)
Stories from Ancient Egypt by Joyce Tyldesley (Oxbow Books, 2012)

Websites
www.ancientegypt.co.uk
www.childrensuniversity.manchester.ac.uk/interactives/history/egypt
egypt.mrdonn.org
www.nms.ac.uk/kids/people_of_the_past/discover_the_egyptians.aspx
Note to parents and teachers: Every effort has been made by the publishers to ensure that these websites are suitable for children. However, because of the nature of the Internet, it is impossible to guarantee that the contents of these sites will not be altered. We strongly advise that Internet access is supervised by a responsible adult.

Places to visit
British Museum, London WC1B 3DG
Manchester Museum, The University of Manchester, Manchester M13 9PL
Museum of Egyptian Antiquities (Egypt Centre), Swansea SA2 8PP

INDEX

THE HISTORY DETECTIVE INVESTIGATES

Contents of all the titles in the series: